The Wright Way to Learn the Piano

THE WRIGHT PIANOFORTE TUTOR

By ALBERT H. OSWALD

Laurence Wright

© 2008 Faber Music Ltd
3 Queen Square, London WC1N 3AU
Printed in England by Caligraving Ltd

ISBN10: 0-571-53176-8
EAN13: 978-0-571-53176-9

A Word to Beginners

By WILHELM BACKHAUS

You will never learn to play the piano unless you love it. I am making the bold statement that everybody loves the piano to begin with. In proof of that, wherever there is a piano in the house you will find all the little ones trying to play it after their own fashion, and taking an obvious pleasure in it.

It is only later on, when they begin to have lessons and are made to play scales and exercises, that that early enthusiasm fades away to some extent. But I hope you will all realise that nothing worth while can ever be achieved without hard work, and that you are not made to play exercises to please your teacher, but because they are the indispensable ground-work to enable you, later on, to give expression to the best that is in you, which is the real object of piano-playing.

In the beginning, you must avoid the excessive use of pedal, as it may easily lead to a slovenly style of playing. On the other hand, as you get more advanced, you will realise that it is just the artistic use of the pedal that gives life, atmosphere and colour to the piano, which would be a cold instrument without it. Further, you must remember that the piano is not only meant to be played, but more particularly to be listened to. Therefore, be careful to listen to yourself most attentively at all times, and be sure that you can hear everything clearly and correctly, and that your ear is never offended by harsh notes. When you have satisfied yourself—that is to say your critical self—it will be the first step towards giving pleasure to the listeners.

The exercise of any art, including piano playing, is, of course, incomplete without the audience to share your pleasure in it, and even if your aim is not to become a virtuoso you will certainly feel that you want to communicate to others what you, yourself, find beautiful. As this is the real object and end, the listener, or the prospective listener, should never be quite lost sight of in all your work on the piano.

A lot is being talked about playing the piano "with expression." Well, I take it for granted that you could not possibly play otherwise if you tried, because you have got a personality and feeling of your own, and could not possibly throw them off just while you played the piano. But do not affect any feeling, just be perfectly natural, and at the same time be reverential towards the works of the great Masters you are trying to perform, then your performance cannot fail to have the stamp of your own personality.

Do not try to make a Beethoven Sonata a medium to express the bad humour you may be in at the time for some reason or other, but let only your best qualities have full rein.

Do not worry too much about what the composer "means" by this or that note. Generally, it is quite impossible to give a name to what he really meant. Music is just an expression of moods which are beyond words to explain. If it were not so, I could "talk" a Chopin nocturne to you instead of playing it.

It is obvious that you must not shut yourself up for eight hours a day practising, as it would damp your enthusiasm. Your playing would become mechanical and you would lose your freshness and the impulse to convey any message to the listener.

I have never practised more than three hours a day. I cannot undertake to say that this would be sufficient for everybody, but I will say that you cannot learn everything just by sitting at the piano. Some inspiration how a certain passage should be played may come to you while taking a walk, or perhaps, while playing tennis, and in that sense I may say that I am working almost day and night, constantly having musical and technical problems on my mind.

If you play technical exercises never do it merely mechanically, and with only half your attention, but play every note with the intensity of your whole personality. Realise that you cannot play the piano well if you cannot play a scale perfectly.

If I quote Schumann: "There is no end to learning." I do not want to discourage you, but merely to point out that the art of piano playing is really infinite. The better you learn to play the more problems will arise, and human life is not long enough to master them all. But there is no greater pleasure than striving after the ideal.

Wilhelm Backhaus

Why You Should Learn to Play the Piano

By HORATIO NICHOLLS

How often you hear someone, who loves music, say, "If only I could play the piano."

They speak that phrase with very real regret, and there is a very real reason for that regret.

Something beautiful has been missed by them, a talent lost, that, with a little patience and work, might have been won.

There is hardly a soul in this country who is conscious of beauty and yet does not love music. The pity of it all is that so few are aware of the real gifts that they possess.

Take the average child for instance. When first the child is able to toddle, his tiny steps lead him towards the piano and his baby fingers pick out the notes.

Instinctively he finds the sounds of them pleasing. Later he may learn, but, through the lack of sympathy of his teacher, or the fact that music is not made interesting enough for him, he never continues.

The talent that might have been gained has been lost.

And what a world of wonder lies in music, and specially in the art of playing the piano.

As a pastime it will keep the most lonely person contented with their own imaginings. *As a pleasure* it will afford a most wonderful happiness to others.

An individual who can play the piano is someone who is sought after as an asset at any social function.

A dull evening can be turned into a time of delight when the piano is being played by someone who knows how to bring out the beautiful harmonies that lie concealed amid the keys and the vibrating strings of that most wonderful of all musical instruments.

There is the other aspect of pianoforte playing.

Often the amateur pianist, in a time of hardship has had, in this asset of piano expertness, the chance of regaining his fortunes with the help of music.

Alas, too many people leave the learning of the piano too late. They wait until there is but scant hope of the dream that they had ever being fulfilled.

One should commence when young, it is true, but the old adage, "It is never too late to mend," applies to the pianoforte as to most other things.

Here, at your disposal, is a method by which you may learn the pianoforte with the experience of an expert musician to aid you.

As long as you have patience to carry out the instructions, and to practice, you will succeed.

There are many systems of pianoforte playing that are designed to teach a pupil in a few lessons.

Alas for the hopes of such a pupil.

Any reasoning individual must know that so glorious a thing as music is something that has to be wooed and won by work and patience.

The only method is to learn by means of a real tutor that makes no sensational claims to teaching you in a few days, but *does* claim to teach you thoroughly in time if you follow its dictates and practice as you are told to practice.

To those who intend commencing a tutorial system of pianoforte playing I can supply the best advice in my power, for, as a composer, one of my greatest ambitions has been to encourage others in an art that has always absorbed me.

I can give you no better hint than that the thing you should first strive to attain is patience to keep on with your studies.

If there was one short and easy road to success I would show you the way to it, but, believe me, patience gives experience and wisdom, in music as in other matters.

You would be well advised to practise systematically and to avoid playing too fast.

"Go slow" is an ideal maxim for the pianist and another excellent precept is to memorise as much as you can.

Learn to love your piano and it will help you more than I can say. If you make a joy of the work it will cease to be work and become a pleasure beyond compare.

As you progress, be careful of your tone qualities and look for the harmonies in all that you play.

Above all things hear as much music as you can, and watch other pianists.

Learn, like better players than yourself, to touch the keys so that you obtain the correct quality of feeling.

Be discriminating in the use of the pedals. Do not thump but rather caress the piano.

I can assure you that once you have grasped the full meaning of this tutor, that once you have entered heart and soul in the task that confronts you, then will you find that with each day the marked improvement will act as a spur to help you on to ultimate success.

It is a fallacy to imagine that you will *never* play the piano. I can, without any equivocation declare, that, following the teaching of this tutor, you *can* play the piano—and *will*.

Horatio Nicholls

RUDIMENTS OF MUSIC.

Musical sounds are expressed by characters called Notes.

The Notes are named after the first seven letters of the Alphabet, namely; A,B,C,D,E,F,G.

The different notes of Music are written on and between the lines of a Stave.

The Stave consists of five lines and four spaces, and these are counted upwards.

Notes are named according to the Clef placed at the beginning of the Stave. In Pianoforte music, two clefs are used, the Treble (or G Clef) and the Bass (or F Clef).

The Treble Clef is placed upon the second line and the Bass Clef is placed upon the fourth line

The two Clefs are joined together by a Brace, thus:—

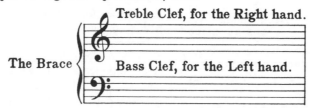

Treble Clef, for the Right hand.

The Brace

Bass Clef, for the Left hand.

Names of the Treble Notes.

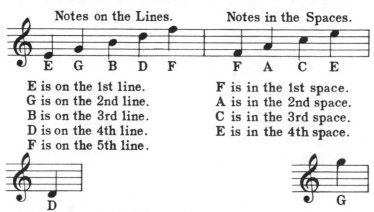

Notes on the Lines.

Notes in the Spaces.

E   G   B   D   F   F   A   C   E

E is on the 1st line.
G is on the 2nd line.
B is on the 3rd line.
D is on the 4th line.
F is on the 5th line.

F is in the 1st space.
A is in the 2nd space.
C is in the 3rd space.
E is in the 4th space.

D

The note under the 1st line is D.

G

The note over the 5th line is G.

When other notes are required both higher and lower than those placed on the lines and in the spaces, short additional lines are used, called Ledger Lines. The Ledger Lines above the stave are counted upwards, and those below the stave are counted downwards.

Treble Notes above the Stave.

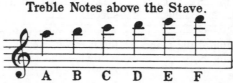

A   B   C   D   E   F

A is on the 1st ledger line above the Treble stave.
B is above the 1st ledger line above the Treble stave.
C is on the 2nd ledger line above the Treble stave.
D is above the 2nd ledger line above the Treble stave.
E is on the 3rd ledger line above the Treble stave.
F is above the 3rd ledger line above the Treble stave.

Treble Notes below the Stave.

C   B   A   G

C is upon the 1st ledger line below the Treble stave.
B is below the 1st ledger line below the Treble stave.
A is upon the 2nd ledger line below the Treble stave.
G is below the 2nd ledger line below the Treble stave.

Treble Notes in Successive Order.

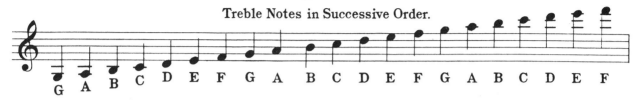

G A B C D E F G A B C D E F G A B C D E F

An Octave is the distance from one note on the piano to the next above or below of the **same name.**

E to E   F to F

Names of the Bass Notes.

Notes on the Lines.   Notes in the Spaces.

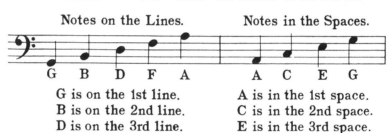

G B D F A   A C E G

G is on the 1st line.   A is in the 1st space.
B is on the 2nd line.   C is in the 2nd space.
D is on the 3rd line.   E is in the 3rd space.
F is on the 4th line.   G is in the 4th space.
A is on the 5th line.

F

B

The note under the first line is F.   The note over the 5th line is B.

Bass Notes above the Stave.

C   D   E   F   G

Bass Notes below the Stave.

E   D   C   B

Bass Notes in Successive Order.

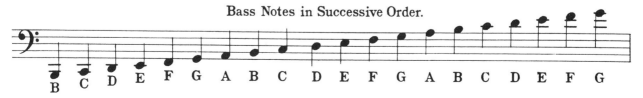

B C D E F G A B C D E F G A B C D E F G

In modern music there are now commonly in use six kinds of notes: their names and forms are as follows:–

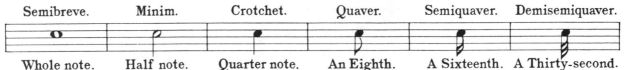

Semibreve.	Minim.	Crotchet.	Quaver.	Semiquaver.	Demisemiquaver.
Whole note.	Half note.	Quarter note.	An Eighth.	A Sixteenth.	A Thirty-second.

The Semibreve 𝅝, a round open note is the longest now in general use.

A Minim 𝅗𝅥, a round open note with a stem, is half the value of a Semibreve, (two Minims equal one Semibreve).

A Crotchet 𝅘𝅥, a black note with a stem, is half the value of a Minim, (four Crotchets equal a Semibreve).

A Quaver 𝅘𝅥𝅮, a black note with a stem and a hook, is half the value of a Crotchet, (eight Quavers equal a Semibreve).

A Semiquaver 𝅘𝅥𝅯, a black note with two hooks, is half the value of a Quaver, (sixteen Semiquavers equal a Semibreve).

A Demisemiquaver 𝅘𝅥𝅰, a black note with three hooks, is half the value of a Semiquaver, (thirty-two Demisemiquavers equal a Semibreve).

The following Table will explain the relative value of the notes.

Table.

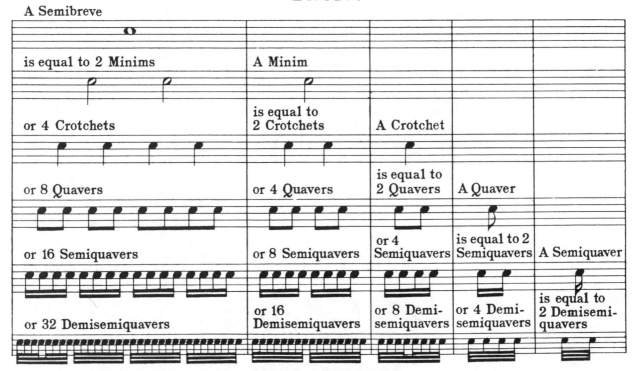

A Dot placed after a Note makes it half as long again.

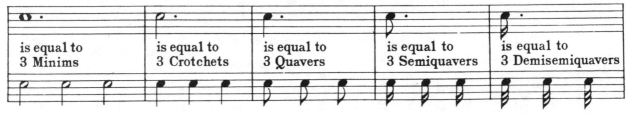

When a Note has two Dots placed after it, the sound is prolonged by three-quarters the value of the Note.

A double dotted Minim	A double dotted Crotchet	A double dotted Quaver
is equal to 3 Crotchets and a Quaver	is equal to 3 Quavers and a Semiquaver	is equal to 3 Semiquavers and a Demisemiquaver

Silence is indicated by signs called **Rests.** Each species of Note has its Rest, which in point of duration is equal to the Note itself.

Semibreve.	Minim.	Crotchet.	Quaver.	Semiquaver.	Demisemiquaver.
Semibreve Rest.	Minim Rest.	Crotchet Rest.	Quaver Rest.	Semiquaver Rest.	Demisemiquaver Rest.

The Semibreve rest is placed under a line of the stave
The Minim rest on a line of the stave
The Crotchet rest turns to the right
The Quaver rest turns to the left
The Semiquaver rest with two hooks turns to the left
The Demisemiquaver rest with three hooks turns to the left

When a Rest occurs, the fingers must be raised from the keys.

One or two Dots after a Rest, lengthen the silence in the same proportion as they would do its corresponding note.

Every piece of music is divided into equal portions of Time, called Measures, by Bars (which are thin strokes) drawn through the Stave, thus:

A Double Bar consists of two thick strokes drawn through the Stave, thus:  and it shows the conclusion of any Air or Movement.

Time signatures are placed at the beginning of a piece.

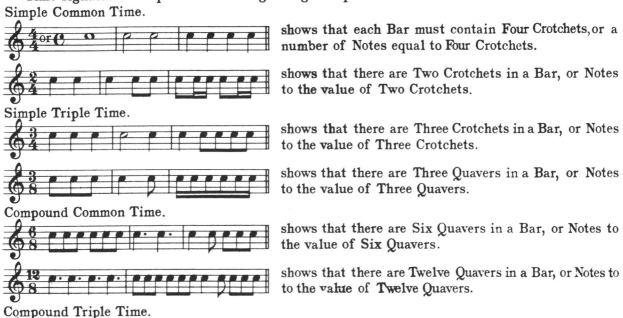

Simple Common Time.

shows that each Bar must contain Four Crotchets, or a number of Notes equal to Four Crotchets.

shows that there are Two Crotchets in a Bar, or Notes to the value of Two Crotchets.

Simple Triple Time.

shows that there are Three Crotchets in a Bar, or Notes to the value of Three Crotchets.

shows that there are Three Quavers in a Bar, or Notes to the value of Three Quavers.

Compound Common Time.

shows that there are Six Quavers in a Bar, or Notes to the value of Six Quavers.

shows that there are Twelve Quavers in a Bar, or Notes to to the value of Twelve Quavers.

Compound Triple Time.

shows that there are Nine Quavers in a Bar, or Notes to the value of Nine Quavers.

THE K

Pupils should study this carefully— it is the e
at the same time it shows y

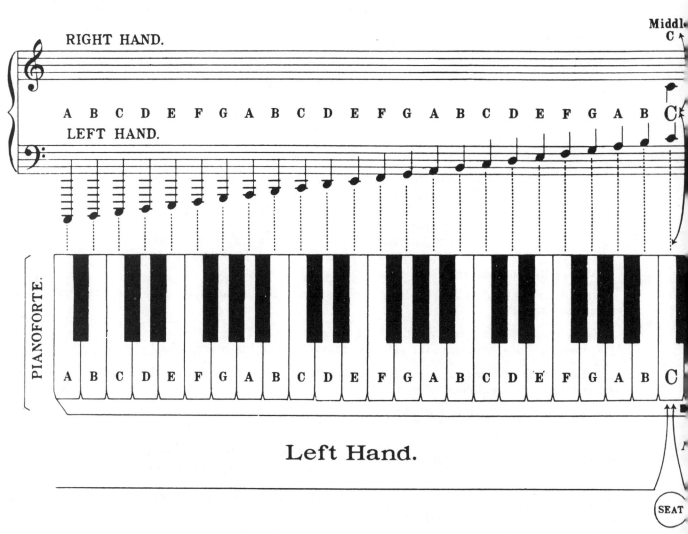

Left Hand.

NOTE— The Middle C is oppos

The Keyboard of the Pianoforte is formed of White and Black Keys. The White Keys represent the natural notes, and the Black Keys are used for the sharps and flats. The Black Keys are divided into alternate groups of two and three. Observe that the White Note on the Left Hand side of every group of Two Black Keys is called C; D is between the Two Black Keys; E is on the right of the Two Black Keys; F is on the left of the Three Black Keys; and G is above the lowest of the Three Black Keys. By bearing the positions in memory no difficulty will occur in finding any note.

-BOARD.

...ay to learn the name of each note on the Piano—
...the notes are written in music.

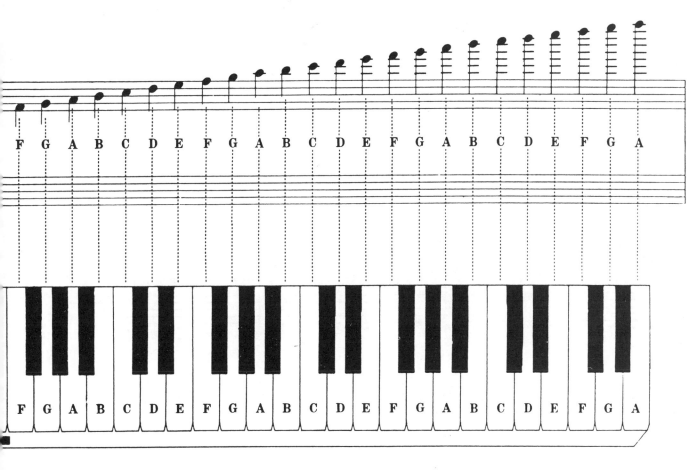

Middle C is at
left of the Lock.

Right Hand.

...tre of Piano Seat.

Position of the Hands.

LEFT HAND   RIGHT HAND.

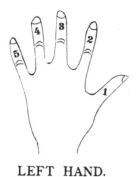

Section of Key-Board.

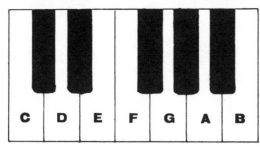

LEFT HAND.

RIGHT HAND.

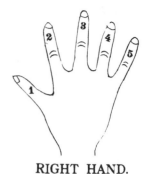

Preparatory Lessons.

The following exercises must be practised slowly, first with the fingers of the Right Hand, and then in a like manner with the Left Hand. When the fingers have become quite accustomed to the notes, the exercises may be played with both hands.

Fingering is expressed in the following manner: 1 stands for the Thumb, 2 for First Finger, 3 for Second Finger, 4 for Third Finger, 5 for Fourth Finger.

Bass Notes: Left Hand Exercises

SHEAF OF MELODIES.
(Treble and Bass)

1. Common Time

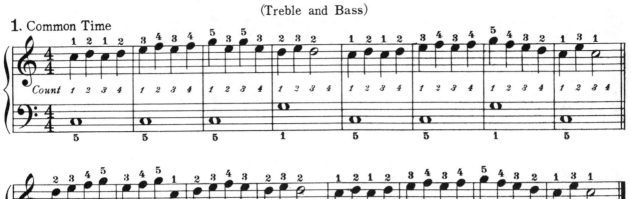

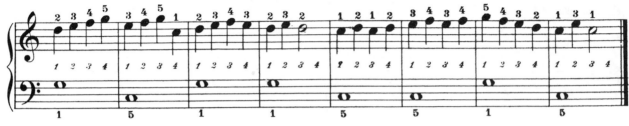

2.

3. Simple Duple Time

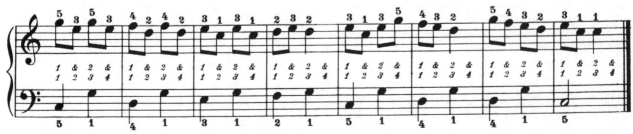

Daily Exercises.

Each of these exercises must be played over six or eight times, slowly at first, with increase of time as the pupil improves.

Double Notes.

Prelude in C Major.

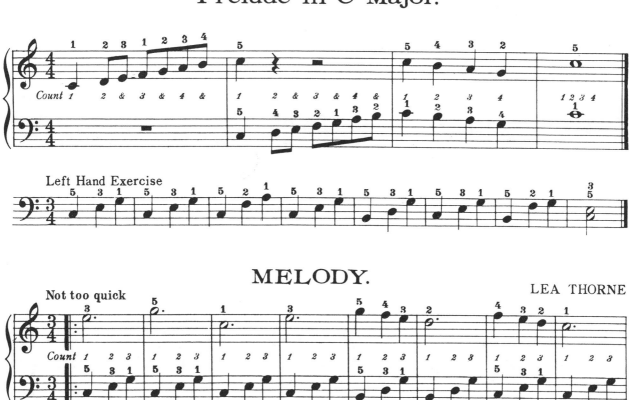

Left Hand Exercise

MELODY.

LEA THORNE

*The dots at the double bar indicate that the music is to be repeated

MARCH.

LEA THORNE

CRADLE SONG.

LEA THORNE

VALSE.

ALBERT H. OSWALD

MARCH OF THE ELVES.

LEA THORNE

HIDE AND SEEK.

Not too quick

SONG.

LEA THORNE

Rather slow

*Da Capo or D.C. implies that the music should be repeated from the beginning. Finish where the word
Fine is placed

SUNNY HOURS.

ALBERT H. OSWALD

Triplets.

A Triplet is a group of three notes of equal value, which are played in the time of two of the same kind; a slur and a figure *3* being placed over, or under the group.

Right Hand Exercise

Sharps and Flats.

The Sharp ♯ raises a white or natural Key a semitone, or one Key higher.

The Flat ♭ lowers a natural note a semitone, or one Key lower.

A Double Sharp ✕ raises a note two semitones. ⎫
A Double Flat ♭♭ lowers a note two semitones. ⎬ Seldom used.

The Natural ♮ restores to its original state any note that has been altered by a Sharp or Flat.

The Key of G Major is known by a sharp. The name of the sharp is F and is placed immediately after the Clef, on the fifth line (F) to show that all the F's must be made sharp.

The **F sharp** is the **black key** just above the **white** or **natural** key F.

Prelude in G Major.

(The F in this Prelude is Sharp)

SNOW FLOWERS.

ALBERT H. OSWALD

L.W.M.Co. 889ª

Left Hand Exercise

SUNSHINE SHOWER.
Valse.

ALBERT H. OSWALD

BANNER OF BRITAIN MARCH.

GORDON VYVYAN

At a swinging pace

EVENTIDE.

LEA THORNE

(1) The notes under or over the slur ⌢ are to be played smoothly
(2) The Sign *8va*-------- signifies that the notes (treble) are to be played an octave, or 8 notes, higher than written

Short Exercise on Tied Notes.

SKETCH.

ALBERT H. OSWALD

*The Bind or Tie under or over two notes which are the *same name* signifies that the second is not to be played, but held down the length of the two

22

Prelude in D Major.
All the F's and C's to be made sharp.

Left Hand Exercise

MERRY MEETING.
GORDON VYVYAN

Moderately quick

MORNING STAR.
Valse.
ALBERT H. OSWALD

★ p for Piano—soft; mf Mezzo forte—moderately loud;
pp Pianissimo—very soft; f Forte—loud;

WITHERED BLOSSOMS.

ALBERT H. OSWALD

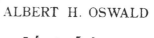

Prelude in A Major.

Three Sharps F♯, C♯ and G♯.

Left Hand Exercise

WINTER ROSES.

ALBERT H. OSWALD

Not too quick

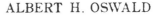

★ Crescendo ⟨ increasing in power of tone
Diminuendo ⟩ gradually diminishing the power of tone

ELFIN GLADE.

ALBERT H. OSWALD

Prelude in F Major.

The Key of F requires one flat B♭

B Flat is the *Black* note on the left hand side of B natural.

Left Hand Exercise

PRIMROSES.
(Mazurka)

GORDON VYVYAN

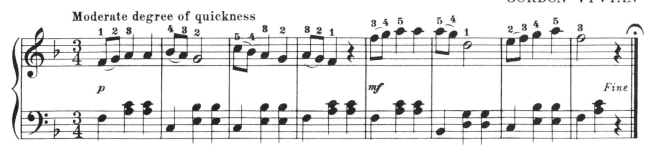

OH DEAR! WHAT CAN THE MATTER BE?

TIT-FOR-TAT.
Schottische.

ALBERT H. OSWALD

BLUE BELL OF SCOTLAND.

Prelude in B♭ Major.

The Key of B flat requires two flats, B♭ and E♭.

STATELY DANCE.

In a graceful style

ALBERT H. OSWALD

CHIME AGAIN BEAUTIFUL BELLS.

R. BISHOP

Prelude in E♭ Major.

The Key of E♭ requires three flats, B♭, E♭, A♭.

★ A Pause 🅟 over a note or rest indicates that it should be prolonged beyond its *actual value*

EVENING STAR.

ALBERT H. OSWALD

TWILIGHT SHADOWS.

LEA THORNE.

★ Rallentando. Gradually slackening the time

STUDY.

LEMOINE

STUDY.

LEMOINE

THE OLD FOLKS AT HOME.

MODERATO.

LEMOINE

*Dots....over or under notes signify that they are to be played Staccato; that is detached, separated; the notes to be short and light

MOON FAIRIES.
Morceau.

ALBERT H. OSWALD

Note change of Key. All F's are natural

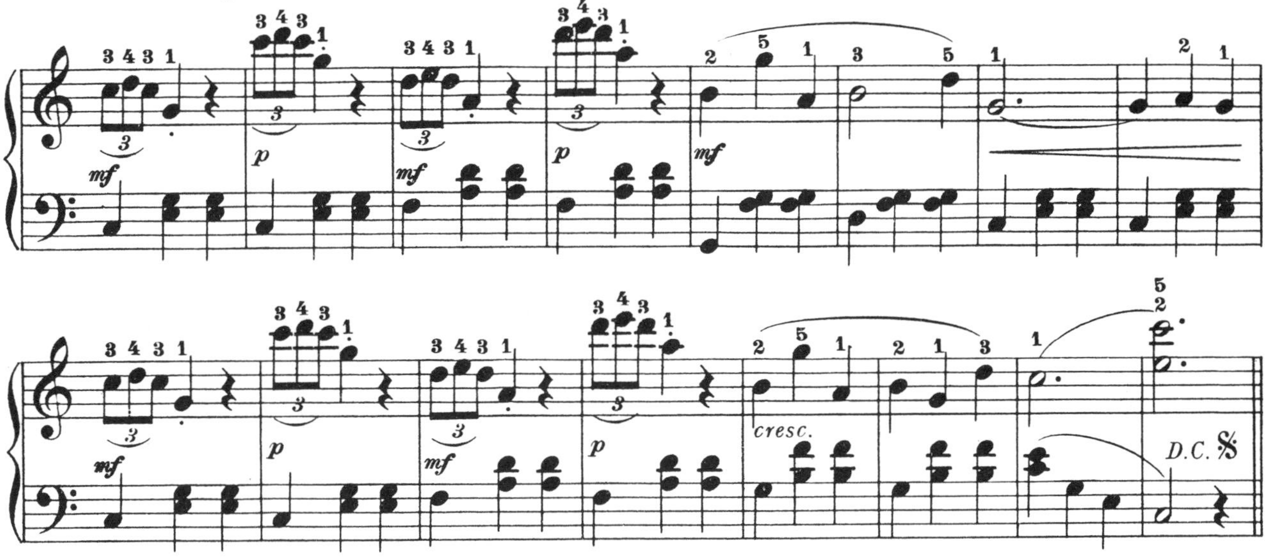

FUN AND FROLIC.

ALBERT H. OSWALD

Con spirito

1st time p
2nd time f

Repeat treble
8va higher

Fine

1st time p
2nd time f

Repeat treble
8va higher

D.C. ℅

*Emphasis ∧ >< give stress to notes so marked

34

MERMAID'S SONG.
Oberon.

BELIEVE ME IF ALL THOSE ENDEARING YOUNG CHARMS.

MOORE

WOODLAND FAYS.

ALBERT H. OSWALD

ALLEGRETTO.

BERTINI

ADESTE FIDELES.

Arranged by
ALBERT H. OSWALD

YORKSHIRE BELLS.

J. PRIDHAM

PURPLE HEATHER.
Gavotte.

GORDON VYVYAN

Note change of Key. All E's are natural

DOUBLE CHANT IN C.

ALBERT H. OSWALD

PLAYTHINGS.

Words by WORTON DAVID

Simplified by ALBERT H. OSWALD

Music by HORATIO NICHOLLS

★ The note B having no black Key adjoining it on the right, the next white key to the right is used as B♯

The note E having no black key adjoining it on the right, the next white key to the right is used as E♯

OMAHA.

Words by WORTON DAVID

Music by HORATIO NICHOLLS

THE MERRY PEASANT.

SCHUMANN

AVE MARIA.

BURGMÜLLER

CHORALE.

ALBERT H. OSWALD.

MORNING HYMN.

ALBERT H. OSWALD.

EVENING HYMN.

ALBERT. H OSWALD.

44

Embellishments and Abbreviations.

The Appoggiatura is expressed by a note in a small character, placed before the principal note. It borrows one-half the value of the principal note, unless that note is dotted, in which case the appoggiatura borrows two-thirds of it.

Double Appoggiatura.

The Acciaccatura (crushing note) has a dash drawn through it thus: ♪ and should be played **smartly** and **quickly**.

The Turn is either direct ∾, or inverted ⸮.

NOTE:– The rapidity of the turn depends upon the time of the movement in which it occurs

The Shake or Trill is marked *tr*⌇⌇⌇ and is played as follows.   A shake generally ends with a turn.

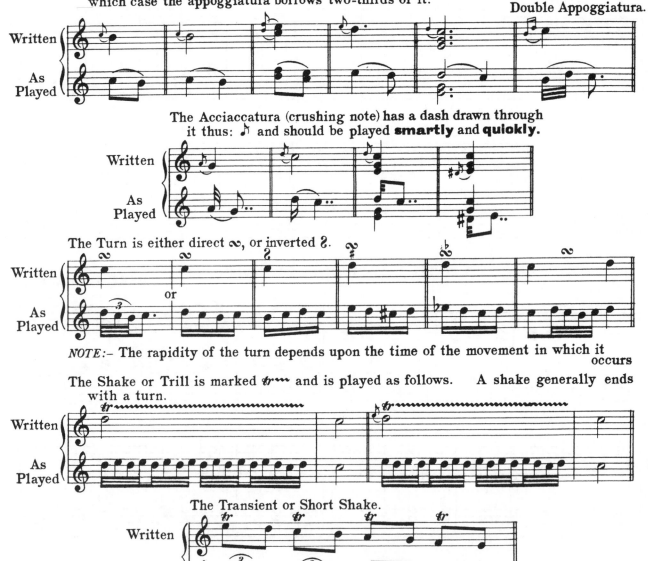

The Transient or Short Shake.

Abbreviations.

The Tremando or Tremolo.

The Waved line ⸾, or the Curved line, thus (when placed before a chord, signifies that the notes are to be played in the Arpeggio style, that is the notes are to be played in rapid succession from the lowest upwards, instead of striking them altogether.

Major Scales.

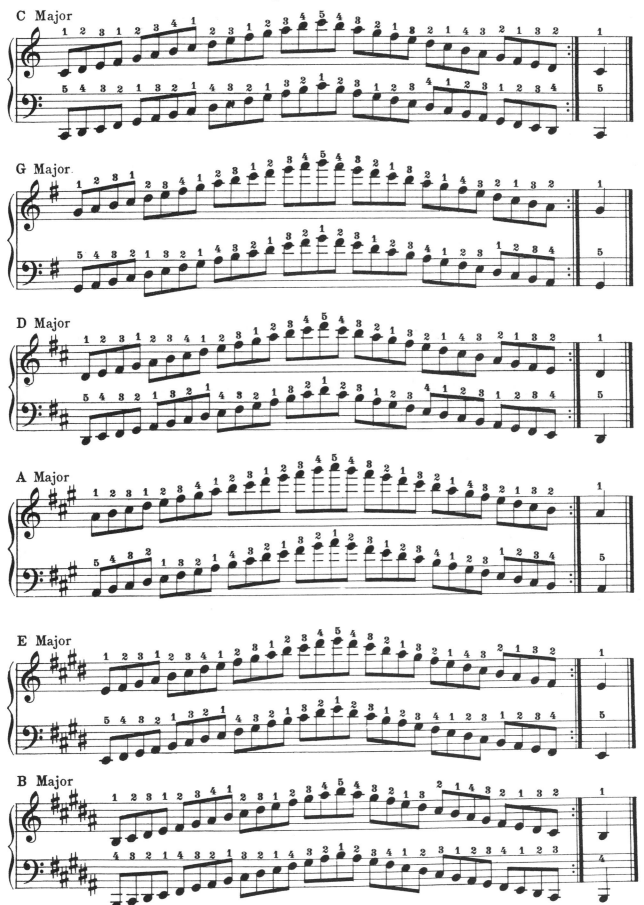

46

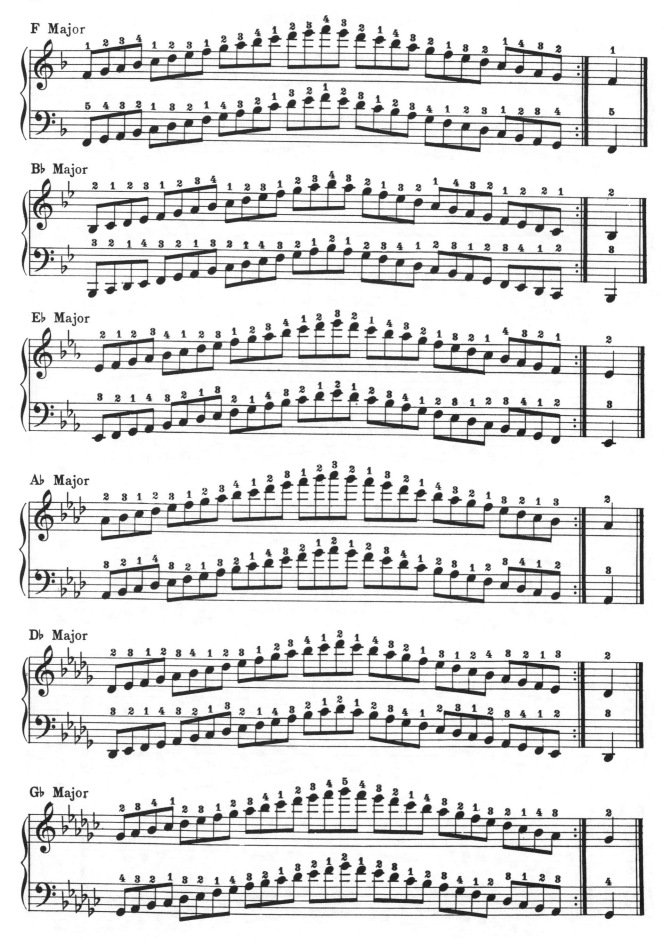

Melodic Minor Scales.

48

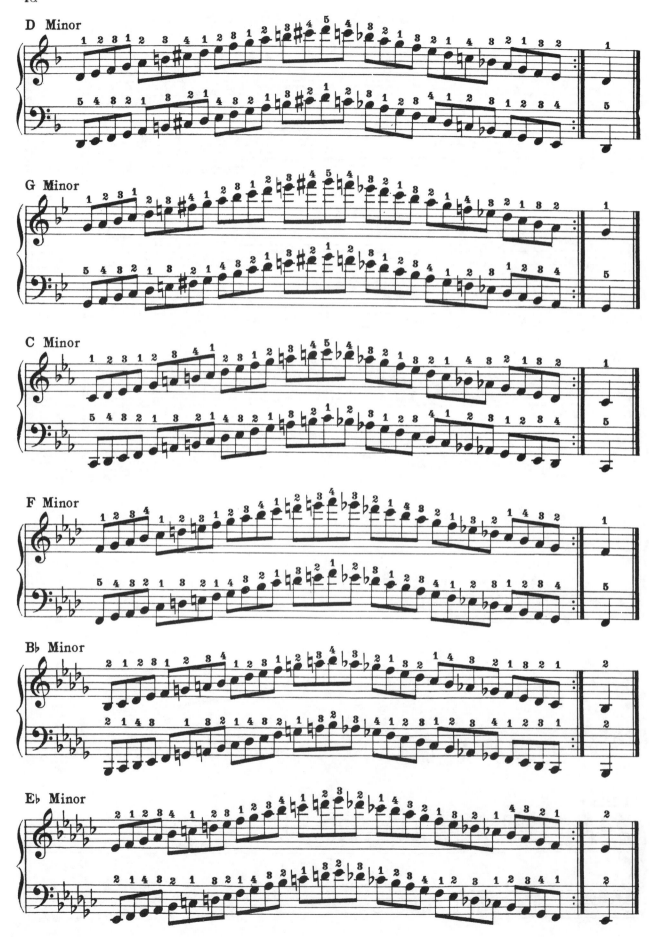

SMOKE RINGS.
Valse.

ALBERT H. OSWALD

HAPPY HOMES.

Pianoforte Duet.

SECONDO.

ALBERT H. OSWALD.

HAPPY HOMES.

PRIMO

ALBERT H. OSWALD

FADING SUNSET.

Pianoforte Duet.

SECONDO.

ALBERT H. OSWALD.

FADING SUNSET.

ALBERT H. OSWALD

PRIMO

SUNBEAMS.

Pianoforte Duet.

SECONDO.

ALBERT H. OSWALD.

SUNBEAMS.

PRIMO

ALBERT H. OSWALD

List of Musical Terms.

Accelerando	Increasing in quickness.
Adagio	Slow.
Adagio Assai	Very slow.
Affetuoso	Tenderly.
Andante	Slow and distinct.
Andantino	A little slower than Andante.
Allegro	Quick, lively.
Allegretto	Rather lively.
Animato	With animation, spirit.
Assai	Very.
A Tempo	In time.
Ben	as Ben Marcato, well marked.
Brillante	Brilliant, showy.
Calando	Gradually diminishing the sound.
Cantabile	In a graceful and singing style.
Chromatic	Proceeding by semitones.
Coda	A special finishing part.
Con Spirito	With spirit.
Crescendo	Increasing the sound gradually.
Dolce	Sweetly, softly.
Diminuendo	Diminishing the sound gradually.
Da Capo (D.C.)	From the beginning.
Di Molto	Very, extremely.
Espressivo	With expression.
Finale	The last movement.
Fine	The end.
Forte (f)	Loud.
Fortissimo (ff)	Very loud.
Forzando (>)	The note is to be marked with force.
Grave	Slow, solemn.
Grazioso	Graceful, elegant style.
Largo	Slow and stately.
Larghetto	Not so slow as Largo.
Lento	Slow.
Legato	Smooth.
Loco	As it is written.
Maestoso	Majestic.
Moderato	In moderate time.
Molto	as Molto Adagio, very slow.
Mezzo Forte (mf)	Rather loud.
Mezzo Piano (mp)	Rather soft.
Non Troppo	Not too much.
Ottava (8va)	An octave higher.
Ottava Bassa	An octave lower.
Piano (p)	Soft.
Pianissimo (pp)	Very soft.
Poco	A little.
Prestissimo	As quick as possible.
Presto	Quick.
Rallentando or Rall.	Becoming slower.
Ritardando or Rit.	Becoming slower.
Risoluto	With boldness and resolution.
Scherzando	Playful, light and sportive.
Sforzando (sfz)	Extra force given to one note.
Sostenuto	Fully sustained.
Staccato	Short, detached.
Stretto	Quicken the time.
Tempo	Time.
Tempo di Marcia	March time.
Tempo di Minuetto	Minuet time.
Tempo Primo	Time as at first.
Tenuto or Ten.	The notes to be held the full value.
Tremolo	With a trembling effect.
Veloce	With rapidity.
Vivace	Lively.
Volti	Turn over.
Volti Subito (V. S.)	Turn over quickly.